CW01431807

Original title:
Jasmine Shutters Among the Dragon Nest

Author: Sara Säde
ISBN HARDBACK: 978-1-80559-317-1
ISBN PAPERBACK: 978-1-80559-816-9

The Blooming Oracle's Lament

In gardens where shadows weep,
The oracle sighs with care.
Petals fall into the deep,
Each whisper lost in the air.

Rains of sorrow kiss the ground,
Silent cries of unseen tears.
Her wisdom wrapped in thorns around,
Echoes traced by fleeting years.

The blooms they sway with fragile grace,
Reflecting stories untold.
In her heart, a sacred space,
Where dreams and memories fold.

Yet time, it weaves a cruel seam,
Worn faces turn to night.
Her voice a faded, fractured dream,
Yearning for morning light.

Among the petals, secrets hide,
In shadows, fate's gentle hand.
The oracle weeps, alone, denied,
In the silence of the land.

Sentinels of the Sylvan Dream

Guardians of the ancient wood,
Branches cradle skies so wide.
Echoes of a world once stood,
Where magic and nature collide.

In moonlit glades where whispers play,
The sentinels breathe the night.
They watch the dance of dusk and day,
Eyes gleaming with timeless light.

With roots entrenched in stories old,
They sway with secrets untold.
In their arms, the wild unfolds,
A tapestry of dreams retold.

Beneath their boughs, soft shadows creep,
Nurtured by the earth's embrace.
In silence, secrets they shall keep,
As stars dance in a celestial chase.

Vows exchanged with the twilight breeze,
In harmony, their spirits sing.
Sentinels sway with effortless ease,
Two worlds bound by the love they bring.

Beneath the Canopy of Mythical Whispers

Underneath the leafy dome,
Whispers float in fragrant air.
Mythical tales reach far from home,
Where magic lingers everywhere.

The creatures of twilight conspire,
To spin tales of old and new.
In shadows cast by the dying fire,
They weave dreams with strands of dew.

Voices echo through the night,
Singing songs of forgotten lore.
Each word a thread, a glowing light,
Binding hearts forevermore.

Leaves tremble as stories pass,
Unfurling paths of fate aligned.
In each heartbeat, echoes last,
Where vision and dream are entwined.

Beneath the canopy's embrace,
The mythical finds a home.
In whispers soft, the world takes place,
As hearts soar free to roam.

Fables Woven in Petal and Scale

In gardens where legends unfold,
Fables bloom in colors bright.
Petals tell of heroes bold,
While scales glimmer in the light.

The creatures of air and earth implore,
Stories spun with threads of fate.
In each whisper, they restore,
The dreams that once did wait.

Tales of love and battles fierce,
Woven in the fabric of night.
In unity, they gently pierce,
The darkness with their radiant light.

Between the blooms, shadows play,
Echoing laughter from the past.
In every heart, a role to sway,
In the stories that were cast.

Fables blend with the softest sighs,
Petal and scale, a dance divine.
Together beneath the endless skies,
They flourish in the world's design.

Tranquility Among the Winged Guardians

In twilight's calm embrace they soar,
Golden rays kiss the forest floor.
Birdsong weaves a gentle thread,
Binding hearts where dreams are fed.

Above the trees, a silent flight,
Feathers flutter, pure delight.
Beneath the sky, soft whispers play,
Guiding souls along their way.

Each shadow dances in the breeze,
Nature hums through ancient trees.
A sanctuary in the air,
Guardian spirits linger there.

The evening glows with pastel light,
Chasing shadows from the night.
With every beat, the world stands still,
A moment captured, hearts fulfill.

In their presence, worries fade,
Peaceful solace now cascades.
Among the winged, we find our song,
A harmony where we belong.

Whispered Promises in Bloom

In gardens rich with life's embrace,
Petals dance with gentle grace.
Whispers float on fragrant air,
Promises made, tender care.

Sunlight spills on vibrant hues,
Each bud holds a world of news.
With every breeze, secrets share,
Of love and hope, beyond compare.

The bees hum sweet, a soft refrain,
Collecting dreams like drops of rain.
In this haven, hearts entwine,
Beneath the blooms, a sacred sign.

When twilight cloaks the garden's peace,
The moonlight whispers, shadows cease.
In silence, vows are softly sown,
In every blossom, love has grown.

So let us wander hand in hand,
In this enchanted, blooming land.
A tapestry of whispered dreams,
United here, more than it seems.

A Canopy of Celestial Dances

Underneath the starlit dome,
Twinkling lights, our cosmic home.
Galaxies swirl in timeless flight,
Painting dreams through endless night.

The moon casts silver on the sea,
Guiding hearts, so wild and free.
Constellations sing their tune,
In a dance beneath the moon.

Whispers of the cosmos call,
Echoing through the darkness' thrall.
With every turn, a story spun,
In the dance where we are one.

As meteor showers grace the skies,
Fleeting moments, silken ties.
In the stillness, our hopes take flight,
A canopy of endless light.

So let us sway in cosmic streams,
Chasing softly woven dreams.
In this vast expanse, we'll find,
A dance that binds both heart and mind.

Festivals of Color in Serpent's Fold

In valleys rich with vibrant dreams,
The world awakes with vivid schemes.
Each color bursts, a joyful sound,
Life ignites in beams unbound.

Spirals dance in nature's flair,
Festivals rise in the warm, sweet air.
As petals scatter, laughter flows,
Every heart within it knows.

The serpent winds through fields of light,
Whispers secrets of day and night.
In every shade, a story told,
Of ancient wisdom folded gold.

From dawn's blush to dusk's embrace,
A celebration of every face.
In unity, our spirits twine,
Festivals of love, intertwined.

So let us gather, hand in hand,
In the colors of this land.
For in each hue, the heart unfolds,
In the serpent's fold, life beholds.

Ties that Bind the Spirited Groves

In whispered winds and swaying trees,
Their laughter mingles with the bees.
Bright colors dance in sunlit rays,
Nature sings in joyful praise.

Through tangled roots and branches wide,
Mysteries lurk, secrets hide.
Each heartbeat echoes, soft and clear,
A bond of spirit, always near.

Beneath the boughs where shadows play,
Dreams take flight at end of day.
Together weaving tales of old,
In every heartbeat, brave and bold.

The forest whispers stories grand,
Of unity in this vast land.
From ancient roots, new life will spring,
The ties of nature—sacred thing.

So gather 'round and feel the weave,
In every sigh, in night, believe.
For in this grove, our spirits find,
The love that binds, the ties that bind.

Chronicle of the Enchanted Pods

In twilight's glow, the pods emerge,
With secrets held, they softly urge.
Beneath the stars, they start to glow,
A tale of wonders yet to show.

Whispers of dreams within each shell,
A magic spun, where stories dwell.
Each heartbeat tells a tale anew,
A dance of past, a journey true.

With rustling leaves, the branches sway,
As ancient songs invite the play.
Through time they travel, soft and bright,
Woven threads of day and night.

Each pod a tale, of love and loss,
In skies of dusk, they bear the cross.
From forgotten realms, they bring forth joy,
Embodying dreams that time can't destroy.

So gather close, hear their refrain,
In every pod, there's joy and pain.
Chronicles shared in gentle art,
A testament to the beating heart.

The Serpent's Kiss on a Flower's Throne

A serpent weaves through petals bright,
With emerald scales that catch the light.
In gardens rich, where shadows play,
It whispers secrets, soft as day.

Upon the throne of blooms so rare,
It leaves a mark with tender care.
Each flick of tongue, a kiss bestowed,
Upon the flower's blossomed road.

As twilight fades, the air grows still,
A magic lingers, sweet and shrill.
In this embrace of earth and sky,
Love's mystery is woven nigh.

With petals soft, the serpent twines,
In nature's dance, where beauty shines.
Together they create a maze,
Of life's enchantment, a wondrous gaze.

So let the kiss be ever known,
In flower's realm, where love has grown.
For in this bond, life's stories blend,
A serpent's kiss, where dreams transcend.

Riddles Born Among the Ferns

Whispers weave through leafy greens,
Secrets hidden where sunlight gleans.
Mossy paths hold tales untold,
As shadows retreat from the bold.

In the hush, a riddle waits,
Nature's dance and chance creates.
Beneath the ferns, dreams take flight,
Beneath the twinkling stars at night.

Twisted roots in tangled grace,
Embrace the mysteries we face.
In the stillness, hear the call,
Of ancient wisdom, shared with all.

Luminescence of the Dawn-kissed Petals

Beneath the blush of morning's light,
Petals glow, the world ignites.
Dewdrops shimmer, soft and bright,
A symphony of colors in sight.

With every hue, a story blooms,
In silent gardens, nature looms.
Fragile beauty, whispers sweet,
Awakening hearts, love's heartbeat.

Nature's brush paints joy anew,
In dawn's embrace, a life imbues.
Amidst the petals, dreams take form,
As day breaks, the spirit's warm.

Cocooned Sanctuaries of the Heart

Within the walls of tender grace,
Safe havens built in love's embrace.
Whispers shared in twilight's glow,
Where secrets hide, and feelings flow.

Through winding paths of softest thread,
Connections woven, unsaid.
In quiet corners, secrets flow,
The heart finds peace, the soul's tableau.

In every heartbeat, trust is spun,
A cocoon formed, two become one.
In stillness held, forever brave,
The sanctuary we create, we save.

Murmurs of the Serene Oasis

In the stillness, waters gleam,
Reflections dance, a quiet dream.
Palm leaves sway, a gentle tune,
Beneath the watchful, golden moon.

Whispers travel on the breeze,
Carrying peace, oh so sweet.
Each ripple tells a story rare,
Of tranquil moments, free of care.

Here, the soul finds solace deep,
In nature's arms, we gently sleep.
A haven where the heart can roam,
In the serene oasis, we find home.

A Floral Embrace at Dusk

The petals close with whispered grace,
In twilight's glow, they find their place.
Colors blend in soft retreat,
Nature's sigh, a calming beat.

Beneath the sky, a gentle hue,
Fragrance lingers, sweet and true.
As shadows lengthen, dreams resound,
In this stillness, magic's found.

The breeze carries a secret tune,
Of night embracing afternoon.
Stars awaken, blink and gleam,
In the garden, life's a dream.

With each flower, a story told,
Of love and passion, brave and bold.
The world exhales, a soft embrace,
In dusk's sweet light, we find our place.

Together here, we weave the night,
In bloom and color, pure delight.
A floral dance, a whispered truth,
In this moment, we find our youth.

Guardians of the Hidden Sanctuary

Amidst the trees, where shadows play,
The guardians watch, both night and day.
With ancient hearts, they stand so tall,
In silence strong, they heed the call.

Branches weave a secret door,
To hidden paths, to tales of yore.
The forest breathes, a sacred space,
Where spirits linger, time's embrace.

Moonlight dances on the leaves,
In this haven, the heart believes.
Soft whispers guide the lost and lone,
To find the path they've never known.

Each creature small, a watchful eye,
Underneath the endless sky.
In unity, they guard the night,
Protecting dreams till morning light.

Through thickets dense, and shadows deep,
These silent sentinels do keep.
A history rich, unseen and grand,
The guardians of this sacred land.

Echoes of the Serpent's Song

In the hush of shadows near the stream,
The serpent sings, a haunting dream.
Each note weaves through the cool night air,
A melody spun with whispered care.

Underneath the silver moon,
The river dances to the tune.
Ripples shimmer, bright and bold,
Tales of magic softly told.

Twisting through the reeds, it flows,
Where every heart feels and knows.
The serpent's song, a lover's call,
Echoes wide to one and all.

In darkness deep, a guiding light,
Drawn by whispers of the night.
The pulse of nature steals the breath,
In twilight's grasp, defying death.

And in the stillness, souls unite,
In the echo of the serpent's flight.
A sacred hymn, both wild and free,
Resonates eternally.

Twilight's Kiss on Gentle Pink

The horizon blushes, softly glows,
As day in tender twilight slows.
A canvas brushed with hues that blend,
Where evening whispers sweetly mend.

Petals drift on warm, soft air,
They dance like dreams devoid of care.
In gentle strokes, the colors flow,
Tidbits of joy, a velvety show.

The sun dips low, a shy goodbye,
A promise kept beneath the sky.
In every hue, a lover's spark,
The world ignites from light to dark.

A symphony of soft, warm light,
Enfolds the shadows, ends the fight.
In this embrace, all fears subside,
As stars emerge, the night, our guide.

Twilight lingers, kisses sweet,
In every heart, this moment's beat.
A treasure found in every wink,
In twilight's kiss on gentle pink.

Starlit Pathways of the Heart

Beneath the stars, where whispers roam,
Hearts entwined, we find a home.
Guided by light, soft and serene,
In pathways starlit, love's unseen.

Echoes of dreams dance on the breeze,
A symphony sung among the trees.
Each step we take, a secret shared,
In these starlit paths, our souls bared.

Moonbeams weave through shadows deep,
As night descends, the world in sleep.
Yet in the dark, our lanterns glow,
A journey through realms only we know.

Together we walk, side by side,
In the embrace of the mystic tide.
With every heartbeat, every breath,
We tread the paths where love finds rest.

So let the starlit skies bear witness,
To the stories wrapped in sweetness.
In the sacred vault of the night,
Our hearts shine bright, a guiding light.

Guardians of the Floral Secrets

In gardens lush, where colors bloom,
The secret keepers dispel the gloom.
With petals bright, and fragrance sweet,
Guardians watch where flowers meet.

Among the leaves, a gentle sway,
Whispered tales of night and day.
Every bud a story told,
In nature's book, both new and old.

Butterflies dance in radiant grace,
While bees hum softly, a sacred space.
Each blossom holds a whispered prayer,
A bond unbroken, pure and rare.

The roots entwine in the soil's embrace,
Connecting lives in a sacred place.
With tender care, we nurture and grow,
Guardians of secrets only we know.

So let us tend to this floral dream,
As nature unfolds its vibrant theme.
Together we stand, hand in hand,
Guardians of the earth, a living band.

Enigma of the Celestial Bloom

In twilight's grasp, a bloom unfolds,
Mysterious petals, stories untold.
Each layer whispers of distant stars,
The enigma of beauty that heals the scars.

Luminous hues paint the evening sky,
As shadows gather and moments fly.
In the garden of dreams, the heart takes flight,
Chasing the echoes of soft starlight.

With every breath, the cosmos sighs,
An invitation to seek and rise.
In the bloom's embrace, the secrets lie,
Awakening hope as night draws nigh.

Amongst the silence of nature's grace,
The celestial bloom finds its place.
An enigma whispered from flower to soul,
In the tapestry woven, we become whole.

So let the night be our guide and friend,
In the realm where beginnings never end.
With each petal's touch, we find our way,
In the enigma of the night and day.

Hidden Sanctum of the Emerald Silence

Deep in the woods, where shadows play,
A hidden sanctum calls to stray.
Emerald leaves and silence reign,
In this embrace, we lose our pain.

Mossy stones and ancient trees,
Whispered secrets carried by breeze.
In this haven, time stands still,
A sacred space where hearts can fill.

Glimmers of light filter through,
Painting dreams in every hue.
Here in silence, we find our voice,
In stillness, we learn to rejoice.

Nature's lullaby softly sings,
As we reflect on what life brings.
With every breath, the calm returns,
In this sanctuary, the spirit learns.

So let the world fade far away,
In the emerald silence, we wish to stay.
For within this sanctum, hope ignites,
A hidden treasure in tranquil nights.

Enigma of the Rustling Leaves

In shadows deep, the whispers flow,
A dance of greens where secrets grow.
They speak of time, of dreams once known,
In every crack, the mysteries sown.

With every gust, a tale unfolds,
Of distant nights and ages old.
The rustling hints at stories bare,
In nature's choir, a hidden prayer.

Beneath the boughs, a world of sighs,
Where spirits linger, softly rise.
The canvas brushed by gentle hues,
In nature's breath, the heart renews.

Through every leaf, a path is drawn,
A fleeting glance, a subtle dawn.
The enigma waits in quiet grace,
In rustling leaves, we find our place.

Tales Woven in Perfumed Air

The lilies bloom, their stories sweet,
In garden paths where lovers meet.
A fragrance lingers, soft and rare,
In whispers low, of dreams laid bare.

The rose unfolds its velvet tale,
While daisies dance in breezes pale.
A tapestry of scents align,
In every breath, a world divine.

From jasmine buds to lavender wave,
Each note a memory, a heart to save.
In perfumed air, the echoes play,
In every sigh, the night turns day.

With petals kissed by morning dew,
The stories weave, forever new.
In fragrant trails, we find our way,
A journey marked by scent's ballet.

Nestled Cradles of Nature's Art

In twilight's hush, the nests are formed,
With twigs and dreams, the heart is warmed.
Each cradle holds a life unseen,
A tiny hope, a world between.

The woven strands of earth and sky,
Embrace the young, as time slips by.
In nature's arms, the gentle sway,
A lullaby for night and day.

The vibrant hues of feathers bright,
Nestled safely, out of sight.
Protection wrapped in warm embrace,
In harmony, they find their place.

With whispers soft, the darkness yields,
In cradles deep, the silence shields.
Nature's art, a tender hold,
In every nest, a story told.

Serene Pathways Through Wildflower Realms

In meadows vast, where colors sing,
The wildflowers dance, a vibrant spring.
Each petal bright, a pathway clear,
In nature's realm, we wander near.

The gentle breeze that stirs the blooms,
Carries the scent of sweet perfumes.
With every step on grassy trails,
The spirit soars, as freedom sails.

Beneath the sky, a canvas wide,
Where dreams and blossoms twine and bide.
Serenity in every glance,
In wildflower realms, we find our chance.

The sunlit paths that warmly guide,
With whispers low and hearts open wide.
Through nature's maze, we drift and roam,
In wildflower fields, we find our home.

Filaments of Light Through the Leaves

In the forest deep and wide,
Sunlight dances, shadows glide.
Cascades of green with radiant hues,
Whisper secrets in the morning dews.

Filaments weave, so fine, so bright,
Nature's brush strokes, pure delight.
Through the branches, a gentle sigh,
Promises where the dreams lie high.

Birds in chorus, soft and sweet,
Beneath the canopy, hope and greet.
Each ray of light a tale to tell,
In this enchanted, leafy spell.

A sunbeam here, a flicker there,
Magic mingled in the air.
With every step on earth so dear,
The filaments of light draw near.

So pause awhile, let worries cease,
In this haven, find your peace.
Breathe the beauty all around,
In the leaves, true joy is found.

Guardians of the Evening's Glow

As daylight fades to twilight's charm,
The stars emerge, the world's calm.
In shadows deep, the soft winds blow,
Guardians rise in evening's glow.

With watchful eyes, they take their place,
In the dusk, a warm embrace.
They guide the dreams that freely roam,
In this sacred, nightly dome.

Whispers of night, cool and clear,
Echo softly, still and near.
Moonlight dances on gentle streams,
Where the guardians cradle dreams.

Their presence felt, though seldom seen,
In the hush where hearts convene.
Each pulse of light, a silent vow,
To keep the night, and here and now.

So close your eyes, let visions flow,
With guardians of the evening's glow.
In their embrace, the world finds rest,
A tranquil night, a time blessed.

The Enchantment of Veils and Wings

In a world where whispers dwell,
Veils of mystery softly swell.
Fluttering wings of colors bright,
Paint the canvas of the night.

Dance of shadows, artful grace,
Each veil a story to embrace.
In the twilight, magic stirs,
Awakening the quiet purrs.

Time flows lightly as the breeze,
Carrying tales from ancient trees.
A gentle touch, a fleeting glance,
In the dusk, the veils entrance.

Moths and fairies, spirits shy,
Drifting softly as lanterns fly.
In this realm where dreams take flight,
Enchantment weaves its veil of light.

So linger here, where wonders sing,
In the magic of veils and wings.
Let your heart take wing and soar,
For in this moment, life is more.

Murmurs of Hidden Blooms at Breathe

In the garden where whispers hide,
Blooming secrets, nature's pride.
Petals soft as evening mist,
In their beauty, we exist.

Murmurs rise from roots below,
In quiet corners, love will grow.
With every sigh, a fragrance swells,
In hidden realms where magic dwells.

Hues of dusk and dawn collide,
In blooms where softest dreams abide.
Colors blend in sweet repose,
The heart's joy, each moment glows.

Listen close, hear nature's song,
In the stillness, where we belong.
Each breath a dance of time and space,
In this haven, a sacred place.

So cherish whispers, soft and sweet,
In hidden blooms, our souls will meet.
With every breath, and every sigh,
Life's gentle murmurs drift and fly.

Secrets in a Serpent's Embrace

In the hush of the night, whispers creep,
Twisted truths that the shadows keep.
A serpent coils, its secrets bare,
In moonlit dance, a silent prayer.

Glimmers of emerald, eyes that shine,
Holding stories, dark and divine.
Beneath the scales, the heart does thrum,
Echoes of ages, secrets become.

Through tangled roots and ancient stone,
In every coil, the past is sown.
A chilling breath, the night grows cold,
The serpent's tale, both fierce and bold.

In twilight's grasp, they wind and weave,
In every shadow, a sigh of leave.
The wisdom lies in silence deep,
In the serpent's grasp, the truths we keep.

So listen close to the whispers low,
Where the serpent's secrets cease to flow.
In the shadows dance, the stories sway,
In an embrace, the night remains gray.

Petals Beneath Gilded Wings

In gardens lush where colors bloom,
Petals flutter, dispelling gloom.
Golden wings above take flight,
A dance of beauty, pure delight.

Softly they land, with grace divine,
Kissed by sun, on verdant vine.
Every whisper, a song of spring,
In the gentle breeze, the blossoms sing.

Yet hidden there, beneath their shade,
Secrets linger, in silence laid.
Each vibrant hue a tale untold,
In petals soft, the heart unfolds.

Gilded wings reflect the sky,
In the twilight, life passes by.
A moment captured, forever stays,
In the dance of petals and sun's warm rays.

So let them fall, unguarded whims,
In nature's dance, where beauty swims.
For beneath the wings, life's layers bind,
In every petal, a truth to find.

Shadows of an Enchanted Grove

In the heart of woods where whispers dwell,
Shadows weave a secret spell.
Trees entwined with mossy grace,
Guarding tales from time and space.

Luminous glows and flickering lights,
Dancing softly in mystical nights.
Beneath the boughs, an age-old lore,
In deepened silence, spirits soar.

Ancient roots curl 'round the past,
In gentle embrace, they hold steadfast.
The air is thick with dreams untold,
In every shadow, a world unfolds.

Time stands still in this sacred place,
Where laughter echoes, and sorrows erase.
Nature hums a sweet refrain,
In the grove's embrace, peace shall reign.

So wander here, let your heart roam,
In the enchanted grove, you find your home.
In the shadows deep, a light will gleam,
As you uncover the grove's hidden dream.

Echoes from the Hidden Glade

In a glade where the wildflowers sway,
Echoes pulse with the close of day.
Nature's breath, a living sigh,
Whispers of old with secrets nigh.

Beneath the boughs, where shadows blend,
Time unwinds, the past descend.
Cool breeze shares forgotten tales,
In every rustle, the memory hails.

Moonlit glimmers on dewdrop's tear,
In hushed tones, we draw near.
Every echo, a fleeting trace,
In the hidden glade, we find our space.

Winds carry laughter, joy and pain,
In every heartbeat, we remain.
A sanctuary where silence reigns,
In the glade's embrace, love sustains.

So linger long where the echoes call,
In the hidden glade, we've known it all.
With every whisper, life's threads entwine,
In nature's heart, our spirits shine.

The Hidden Symphony of Nature's Nest

In the whispers of the leaves, a song is spun,
Gentle breezes carry tales, from dawn till sun.
Nestled within branches, life begins to soar,
Harmony of nature, forever to explore.

Birds trill their melodies, a joyous refrain,
Amongst the blossoms bright, a sweet serenade.
Crickets join the chorus, under the moon's light,
The hidden symphony, a magical delight.

In shadows of the trees, secrets softly hum,
The rustle of the grass, where rhythms come from.
Nature's true composition, so seamlessly spun,
A concert of existence, beneath the golden sun.

Each note a gentle whisper, each chord a tender sigh,
The melody of life, in every fluttering sky.
Creating bonds unspoken, in the quietest spaces,
The hidden symphony lives, in all of nature's bases.

Petals Cradled in Artful Shadows

Beneath a canopy, where soft colors lie,
Petals whisper secrets, to the passing sky.
Cradled by the twilight, in moments where they stay,
Artful shadows dance, as daylight fades away.

Orchid blooms like lanterns, glowing in the night,
Magnolia dreams unfolding, soft and pure delight.
Each blossom tells a story, draped in evening's grace,
In this realm of shadows, beauty finds its place.

Lush gardens painted gently, in hues of deep desire,
Lilies quiver quietly, like hearts that never tire.
In silence, petals shimmer, beneath soft starlit gleam,
Cradled in artful shadows, they drift in a dream.

The scent of dew-kissed blossoms fills the midnight air,
A melody of fragrance, of love so soft and rare.
Petals cradled softly, in nature's tender thrall,
Artful shadows weave, a delicate enthrall.

Loops of Life in the Verdant Net

In verdant nets of green, where cycles weave and flow,
Life dances in the sunlight, with movements soft and
slow.
Roots intertwine like stories, beneath the earth's embrace,

Loops of life unbroken, in this thriving space.

Frogs leap in the marshlands, water's gentle sigh,
While flowers bloom like laughter, reaching toward the
sky.
Leaves whisper ancient wisdom, as winds begin to swell,
The loops of life continue, in nature's endless spell.

Where gentle streams keep flowing, weaving tales from
the past,
Each drop a silver echo, of moments made to last.
The cycles of the seasons, in a waltz of time and grace,
Loops of life unveil, in the wilderness's embrace.

Among the towering forests, where ancient spirits blend,
Life drapes its vivid patterns, as beginnings meet their
end.
In the quiet presence, of this earthly rendezvous,
The loops of life encircle, in vibrant shades anew.

The Enchanted Veil of Floral Secrets

Beneath the emerald leaves, a tapestry unfolds,
An enchanted veil of whispers, where nature's heart
beholds.
Petals soft as moonlight, secrets held so dear,
Floral beauty flourishes, in the softest atmosphere.

Roses blush with laughter, jasmine hums a tune,
Lilies weave together, stories of the moon.
Climbing vines embrace the walls, in a gentle, warm
caress,
The enchanted veil conceals, a world of tenderness.

Buds in their tight slumber, waiting for the dawn,
Unfold their hidden tales, as the light is drawn.
Each bloom a quiet message, carried by the breeze,
Floral secrets linger, hidden 'neath the trees.

In the quiet of the garden, life finds its gentle pace,
An enchanted veil that cradles, nature's pure embrace.
Keeping close the stories, of winds that sigh and sing,
Floral secrets blossoming, in the joy of early spring.

The Lure of the Mystical Vines

In shadows deep, the whispers sway,
Entwined in dreams where secrets play.
Vines curl and twist, a fragrant thrill,
Pulling us close, the night is still.

Beneath the stars, a hidden trail,
Guides the heart where wonders unveil.
Each leaf a story, a tale of old,
In nature's grasp, the magic unfolds.

A gentle breeze, the vines respond,
With voices soft, they sing and bond.
Inviting souls to dance and weave,
In the enchantment, we believe.

Moonlight weaves through emerald hue,
Casting spells as if on cue.
A tranquil song calls forth the night,
In the embrace of lovely light.

Together lost in nature's trance,
We sway along, in timeless dance.
The mystical vines embrace us tight,
Forever captured in their light.

Veils of Twilight in the Canopy

As daylight fades, the colors blend,
Veils of twilight, softly descend.
In leafy halls where shadows play,
Secrets linger, just out of sway.

The whispering leaves begin to sing,
A melody sweet, the heart takes wing.
In dusky light, the world transforms,
Where magic in silence gently warms.

Beneath the boughs, the dreams take flight,
Carried aloft by the soft twilight.
A tapestry woven with threads of gold,
In the twilight's arms, stories unfold.

The stars peek down through the verdant dome,
Each flicker a wish, a journey home.
The canopy sways, a gentle embrace,
Where time stands still, and fears efface.

In this sacred space, we find our pause,
In twilight's glow, we'll take our cause.
Carried by whispers of the night,
In harmony found, our souls take flight.

Dance of the Serpent's Melody

In moonlit glow, the serpent sways,
A dance of grace, in silken gaze.
With rhythm divine, it winds and curls,
Weaving through shadows, in swirling whirls.

Each flick of the tail, an ancient sign,
In nature's breath, the stars align.
The echoes of whispers travel far,
In the pulse of the night, we find our star.

Around the fire, the spirits rise,
In the dance of life beneath the skies.
The serpents glide with splendid ease,
A haunting tune that sways the trees.

In every twist, an invitation shared,
To join the dance, if one is dared.
A symphony played by earth and sky,
Where the heartbeats echo and spirits fly.

So let the melody guide your feet,
In nature's rhythm, feel the beat.
As serpent whispers enchant the night,
In the dance of life, find your light.

Blossoms and Scales in Harmonious Union

In gardens rich where colors bloom,
Blossoms fragrant dispel all gloom.
Among the petals, scales do gleam,
A union formed in nature's dream.

The gentle serpent weaves through flowers,
In harmony shared, they share the hours.
Each petal soft, each scale a light,
Together they dance, a beautiful sight.

Amidst the green, life intertwines,
With grace and beauty, love defines.
The fragrance of spring, the shimmer of scales,
In every whisper, the heart prevails.

Where blossoms sway in softest breeze,
The serpent lounges, at perfect ease.
Nature's canvas painted bright,
In this union, everything's right.

So let us celebrate this sacred blend,
Of scales and blossoms, hand in hand.
Together they flourish, an endless song,
In the heart of nature, where we belong.

The Whispers of Ancient Wings

In twilight's hush, they take to flight,
Ancient wings that pierce the night.
Soft murmurs dance on the cool breeze,
Echoes of time through swaying trees.

Beneath the stars, tales softly spun,
Of battles lost and journeys won.
Together they weave a tapestry,
Of forgotten dreams and mystery.

With every flap, a story shared,
In the stillness, souls are bared.
They carry whispers from afar,
Guiding hearts like a distant star.

The moonlight bathes them in a glow,
As winds of time begin to flow.
In their shadows, secrets hide,
Of epochs past, where legends bide.

So listen close, the night will sing,
To those who dream and feel the sting.
For in the dark, with grace they soar,
The whispers of wings forevermore.

Guardian Blossoms and Serpent Eyes

Amid the thorns, the blossoms bloom,
Soft petals break the grip of gloom.
With every hue, a promise fair,
Guardians watch with vigilant care.

Among the leaves, serpents lie low,
In shadows deep, their secrets flow.
With eyes like jewels, they seek to find,
The pulse of life, both fierce and kind.

Blossoms sway, beneath the gaze,
Of ancient beings in a haze.
Unraveling tales of love and strife,
In every bud, a fragment of life.

Through sunlit days and moonlit eves,
The keeper's watch never deceives.
Roots entwined in whispered lore,
Guardians stand forevermore.

So tread with care through this domain,
For beauty hides both joy and pain.
In the dance of life, hope's embrace,
Guardian blossoms find their place.

Sun-Blessed Canopies of Mystery

Under canopies, where shadows play,
Golden beams pierce through day.
Leaves dance lightly, secrets unfold,
An emerald world of stories told.

With every rustle, magic swirls,
In soft whispers, the forest twirls.
Petals drift like thoughts unchained,
Each moment cherished, never waned.

Sun-dappled paths beckon near,
A journey painted, crystal clear.
In twilight's arms, dreams ignite,
The mystery shimmers in soft light.

Wild hearts wander in hushed bliss,
Finding peace in a gentle kiss.
Through ancient trees, life's rhythm flows,
In the sun's spell, the magic grows.

So let your spirit freely roam,
In this haven, feel at home.
Beneath the sun, where dreams align,
A canopy where hearts entwine.

Radiance Beneath the Rose-Hued Veil

Beneath the veil, where dreams take flight,
Rose hues blush the edges of night.
Every glimmer, a promise bright,
Awakens hope, dispels the fright.

Gentle whispers call the brave,
To dance along the silver wave.
In every corner, wonder hides,
Where shadows mingle, and beauty bides.

With every breath, a new dawn breaks,
In tender moments, the heart awakes.
Through petals soft and silken grace,
A dance of light, a warm embrace.

The world unfolds like a silken thread,
Woven with love, where the lost are led.
In every layer, layers reveal,
Radiance found beneath the veil.

So gaze and seek, for you shall find,
Beauty crafted, intertwined.
Beneath the radiant sky's reveal,
A world of magic, forever real.

The Harmonious Lament of Nesting Hearts

In the twilight's tender embrace,
Whispers of love softly trace.
Beneath the stars, two souls entwined,
In shadows of silence, they find.

Echoes of laughter, distant and near,
They speak in a language only they hear.
Each beat of the heart, a gentle refrain,
In the dance of their joy, a hint of pain.

A nest built from dreams and fragile sighs,
Hopes woven tight under twilight skies.
Yet the winds of fate may shift and sway,
Still, they cling to love, come what may.

The moonlight spills on the ground so bare,
Casting shadows of memories laid bare.
Through trials faced and moments rare,
The song of their souls fills the air.

In the quiet night, a promise is made,
With each heartbeat, their fears will fade.
Together they weave a tapestry bright,
In the harmonious cheer of love's gentle light.

The Serpent's Soft Gaze in Solitude

In the depths of the emerald leaves,
A serpent lies where stillness weaves.
Its gaze, a whisper, soft and low,
In solitude's grasp, it begins to glow.

The sun filters through the tangled vine,
Creating patterns, a dance so fine.
In silence, it watches the world shift,
With patience, the shadows slowly drift.

Every rustle ignites a spark,
In the heart of the forest, a sacred park.
With wisdom ancient, it bides its time,
In the stillness, it finds its rhyme.

Secrets hidden in nature's embrace,
The serpent holds a timeless grace.
In its soft gaze, the truth unfolds,
A story of solitude, waiting to be told.

With each passing hour, the world seems new,
In the depths of the green, where dreams pursue.
The serpent, a keeper of moments fleeting,
In the silence, life's pulse is beating.

Serene Reflections in Nature's Fold

In the morning light, a river runs clear,
Through valleys deep where echoes appear.
Waves of serenity kiss the shore,
In nature's arms, my spirit will soar.

Mountains stand tall, guardians of peace,
Their silent lessons, a sweet release.
With every breeze, a whisper flows,
In the dance of the leaves, tranquility grows.

Birds take flight in joyous delight,
Painting the sky, a beautiful sight.
In their song, the heart can find,
A moment of solace, a tie that binds.

Beneath the trees, shadows play,
In the quiet dusk, I long to stay.
Reflections ripple across the lake,
In the stillness, creation's awake.

With each sunset, the world ignites,
A canvas of colors, enchanting sights.
Nature whispers softly, unfolding truth,
In serene reflections, the magic of youth.

The Secret Chamber of Feathered Dreams

In the boughs of an ancient tree,
A chamber of dreams waits silently.
Feathers of colors, soft and bright,
Whisper of stories hidden from sight.

Nestled within, whispers of song,
Echo through branches, where dreams belong.
With each gentle rustle, secrets seep,
In the heart of the wood, dreams softly creep.

Hushed tales of journeys, far and wide,
In the secret chamber, where hopes abide.
Glimmers of starlight dance on the floor,
Awakening dreams, begging for more.

The world outside, a distant refrain,
While inside, a universe without pain.
With wings of imagination, they soar,
In the chamber of dreams, forever they explore.

With each flutter, a mystery glows,
In the soft dusk where the moonlight flows.
The secret chamber, a haven supreme,
Cradles the heart in a blanket of dreams.

Echoes from the Green Enclave

In the hush of the grove, whispers dance,
Leaves flutter softly, caught in a trance.
Sunlight spills gold on the vibrant hue,
Nature's sweet song in each dew-kissed view.

Moss carpets the ground, a verdant embrace,
Creatures skitter by, moving with grace.
Branches entwined like stories once told,
In the heart of the peace, life unfolds.

Ferns bow low, their secrets held tight,
While shadows play games in the fading light.
Every rustle and sigh, a tale on the breeze,
Echoes of magic hidden in trees.

Rivers hum softly, carving their way,
Guided by stars in the onset of day.
Footprints of wanderers linger and fade,
Within the green enclave, dreams are displayed.

Here time stands still, in a silent embrace,
Memories linger, no need for a trace.
Amongst the old roots, where stories are spun,
Echoes resound till the day is done.

Secrets of the Glistening Thorns

In shadows they bloom, thorns hold their keep,
Glistening jewels where silence runs deep.
Unraveled mystique in petals of night,
Secrets are whispered, hidden from sight.

With every soft touch, a sharpness is found,
Beauty and danger in delicate sound.
The fragrance they breathe, a bittersweet song,
Alluring and fierce, where hearts can belong.

Beneath the bright moon, the thorns softly weave,
Tales of the brave and those who believe.
Lost in the garden where dreams take their flight,
Secrets held close in the heart of the night.

A heart can be pricked, yet love still can grow,
Amidst the sharp thorns, bright blooms overflow.
In a twilight embrace, every story may mend,
Finding strength in the paths that we tend.

So cherish the thorns, let their story unfold,
In each glistening petal, a secret retold.
For in the fine balance of light and of dark,
Glistening thorns carry each flickering spark.

The Garden of Celestial Spins

Stars twinkle softly in the night's gentle sway,
While dreams in the garden begin to play.
Where the cosmos bends low, the flowers do bloom,
In whispers of stardust, they dance and consume.

Moonbeams paint silver on each vibrant leaf,
Time flows like water, a timeless belief.
Planets align in a waltz up above,
The garden's allure, a tapestry of love.

Petals like planets, they spin in delight,
Lost in the magic of ethereal light.
Each blossom a story, in spirals they rise,
The garden breathes life under vast, open skies.

Breezes carry secrets from realms far away,
In melodies spoken by night and by day.
Through the celestial spins, hearts start to soar,
In this sacred place, we always want more.

Forever we wander in the glow of the night,
Where the garden's embrace holds our dreams ever tight.
Each twirl in the starlight, a dance to transcend,
The garden of spins, where beginnings won't end.

Nestled Dreams of the Feathered Realms

High up in the treetops, whispers take flight,
Nestled dreams shimmer in the soft morning light.
Feathers of brilliance, a delicate grace,
Floating on wishes, they drift and embrace.

Songs of the dawn bring the world into view,
Each chirp a reminder of dreams tried and true.
In the heart of the chorus, stories that blend,
Nestled dreams soar, no need to defend.

Rustling leaves cradle the hopes in their arms,
Guardians of dreams, with nature's sweet charms.
Birds dance on breezes, weaving the lore,
In their flights of fancy, our spirits can soar.

Through canopies lush, where shadows entwine,
Moments are gathered like wild vintage wine.
Nestled dreams beckon the hearts left to roam,
In the feathered realms, we find our true home.

As twilight descends, the stars shine with glee,
Carrying whispers of what's yet to be.
In the circle of life, where trails intertwine,
Nestled dreams of the feathered realms always shine.

Enveloping Essence of the Occult Garden

In shadows deep, where secrets sway,
Whispers grow in dusk's embrace.
Petals dark, in silence play,
Every breath a hidden trace.

Twisted roots of ancient lore,
Dance beneath the silver moon.
Mystic lights ignite the floor,
Nature's secrets sing their tune.

Glimmers of an unseen world,
In twilight's grasp, they softly breathe.
From petals dark, the magic swirled,
In every corner, they bequeath.

Lost in time, the souls entwine,
Gardens whisper, shadows meet.
In this space, all hearts align,
Finding peace in twilight's heat.

Through the leaves, the night unfolds,
Silent truths in echoes blend.
In the garden, mysteries hold,
The essence of the night, our friend.

The Serpent's Heartbeat Beneath the Soil

In the earth, a pulse resides,
Rhythm deep, it calls the night.
Secrets murmur, darkness hides,
Serpent slumbers, poised in fright.

Roots entangled, whispers creep,
Tender vines hold stories old.
A restless being, dreams so deep,
Woven tales, in soil, unfold.

Crimson glint of ancient scales,
Beneath the weight of timeless stone.
Nature's keeper, woven trails,
To guide the lost towards their own.

When storms do break and silence brews,
The heartbeat quickens, earth does sigh.
In shadows cast, the wisdom chews,
The serpent's heart beneath the sky.

Awakening the world at dawn,
With every shiver, life begins.
So watch the dance of dusk till dawn,
For nature's song is true within.

A Tangle of Colors Wrapped in Silence

In a realm where silence speaks,
Colors blend in gentle dance.
Petals brush like softest cheeks,
In hidden dreams, they find their chance.

A tapestry of light and shade,
Brushes stroke the canvas wide.
Every hue a soft cascade,
Wrapped in whispers, worlds collide.

In stillness, portraits intertwine,
Frames of stories lost to time.
The oracle of blooms divine,
Suggests the muted, quiet rhyme.

Through the chaos, beauty's found,
In each layer, tales persist.
Wrapped in silence, life unbound,
The brush of twilight paints a twist.

Hidden worlds behind the veil,
Tangle blooms, enchant the heart.
In silence, color's gentle trail,
Leads the dreamer to depart.

Glimmering Echoes of Soothing Breeze

In the glade where whispers flow,
Breezes weave through open space.
Softly, leaves in twilight glow,
Echoing the stars' embrace.

Patterns dance in silver light,
Winds of calm caress the face.
Every breath, a sweet delight,
Nature's sigh, a soft embrace.

Glimmers born from starlit dust,
Touch the spirits resting near.
Breezes speak as shadows trust,
In the night, their tales appear.

Through darkened paths of ancient trees,
Gentle hands of night do weave,
Soft are calls of wandering breeze,
In this calm, the heart believes.

Awake, the world in whisper's grace,
Touch the stars, let silence reign.
In echoes, find your quiet place,
As soothing breezes break the chain.

A Tapestry of Winged Guardians

In twilight's glow, they take their flight,
Feathers glinting, catching light.
With silent grace, they guard the night,
Nature's whispers, their guiding right.

Through ancient boughs, their shadows weave,
Crafting dreams we dare believe.
Echoes soft, the winds perceive,
In their watch, our hopes retrieve.

Beneath the stars, the secrets hum,
To distant realms their hearts succumb.
Each flapping wing a soft drumming,
A symphony of night that's coming.

With every dawn, they fade from view,
Yet in our hearts, they leave their cue.
In nature's arms, the bond is true,
A timeless dance, forever new.

The tapestry they've spun so wide,
In colors bright, our fears abide.
With winged guardians by our side,
In wild embrace, we find our stride.

Tales of the Sylvan Guardian's Watch

In emerald glades, they softly tread,
With wise eyes bright, where magic's bred.
Their stories sung in breezes spread,
The sylvan guardian's path is led.

Amidst the trees, a whisper flows,
Of hidden realms where time bestows.
Each leaf, a tale the forest knows,
Of ancient hearts that nature grows.

Beneath the moon, their vigil stays,
Listening to the forest's ways.
In every branch, a voice that plays,
Guardians of twilight's gentle maze.

As dawn breaks forth, they take their flight,
Through woven dreams and fading night.
In every shadow, soft delight,
They guide the wandering hearts in sight.

With hands outstretched to greet the morn,
They honor all the dreams reborn.
In sylvan glades, a world adorned,
Where every heart feels love's sweet thorn.

Among the Essence of the Heart-Wing

In realms where whispers intertwine,
The heart-wings flutter, soft and fine.
Embraced by light, they brightly shine,
The essence hides where love aligns.

Each beat a story, every sigh,
Resounding through the endless sky.
In golden hues, their spirits fly,
Reminding us of dreams to try.

Amongst the flowers, laughter dwells,
In petals' dance, a force compels.
Through fragrant paths, the magic swells,
A tapestry of time that tells.

When shadows loom, their light remains,
In heart-wings' grace, no fear retains.
Through every trial, joy sustains,
A melody that love ordains.

Among the essence where dreams converge,
In unity, our voices urge.
With heart-wings filled, our spirits surge,
In every soul, their tales emerge.

Petal-Laden Paths of Arcane Whispers

Upon the ground, where petals lay,
A carpet bright, they softly sway.
In whispered tones, the secrets play,
A dance of light, through night and day.

Each step we take, the magic blooms,
In chanted winds, where spirit looms.
Arcane whispers, the heart consumes,
In fragrant paths, the wonder zooms.

Through twilight's veil, enchantments call,
With every petal, fears must fall.
The paths weave tight, a sacred thrall,
Where nature's breath unveils it all.

In shadows deep, a promise gleams,
As moonlight weaves through waking dreams.
With every heartbeat, life redeems,
In petal-laden love's sweet schemes.

Within this realm, we find our truth,
In every step, the pulse of youth.
Arcane whispers, a living booth,
Where hearts can dance, reclaim their roots.

Veils of Petals Among gentle Flows

Veils of petals drift and sway,
In gentle flows where shadows play.
Soft whispers kiss the morning air,
Nature's beauty, beyond compare.

Colors blend in perfect light,
Dancing softly, a pure delight.
Each bloom tells a story true,
A canvas bright, in every hue.

With each breeze, a secret told,
Of warmth and life, and love of old.
Petal by petal, dreams take flight,
In this garden, colors bright.

The sun cascades through leaves and boughs,
Awakening the earth with vows.
In stillness, all the world can feel,
The magic nature's hands reveal.

So let the petals softly fall,
Among the streams that gently call.
Veils of petals, soft and light,
Embrace the day, embrace the night.

Circles of Life Encased in Greenery

Within the leaves, a world does grow,
Circles of life, in sun's warm glow.
Roots entwined in tranquil earth,
Whispering tales of life and birth.

Branches stretch in gentle grace,
Holding secrets in their embrace.
Underneath the canopies green,
Life dances in the spaces between.

Each cycle turns, as seasons change,
Flora and fauna, all rearranged.
In harmony, they weave their fate,
Circles of life, a bond so great.

Through time and space, the stories flow,
In every seed, in every grow.
Nature's hand, a master design,
In this tapestry, we intertwine.

So walk beneath the leafy veins,
Feel the pulse, the heart that reigns.
Encased in greenery, life unfolds,
A timeless tale that nature holds.

The Silent Watchers of Floral Dreams.

In the stillness of the night,
Silent watchers hold their light.
Lilies close, yet dreams remain,
Echoing softly, like gentle rain.

Stars above, like petals rare,
Glinting softly in the air.
Each blossom, a whispered prayer,
In slumber's grasp, they wander there.

The moon casts shadows, faint and bright,
On the edges of dreams in flight.
Silent watchers, ever near,
Guarding hopes, dissolving fear.

Through fragrant air, the magic weaves,
In floral dreams, the heart believes.
Fleeting moments, forever kept,
In the silence, the blossoms slept.

They share their secrets, softly spun,
Of heartbeats lost, and love once won.
The silent watchers hold the scene,
In the garden where dreams convene.

Whispers Through the Lattice

Whispers serenade the morning light,
Through lattice frames, a lovely sight.
Vines entwined with tender grace,
Softly swaying in their place.

Petals blush in shades of dawn,
As nature's breath is gently drawn.
Through the lattice, secrets flow,
In this sanctuary, love does grow.

Birds sing sweetly, notes collide,
In harmony, where hearts abide.
Each rustle shares a voice of peace,
In every crevice, tensions cease.

The sunlight filters, warm and bright,
Painting patterns, pure delight.
Whispers dance like dreams in air,
In lattice shadows, free from care.

So pause awhile, let silence bloom,
Through whispers, find your heart's true room.
In this embrace of flora's grace,
Let every moment leave a trace.

Whispering Blooms in Twilight

In the hush of night, flowers sigh,
Petals dance softly under the sky.
A gentle breeze carries their tune,
While shadows embrace the glowing moon.

Whispers of color in fading light,
Gold and purple, a breathtaking sight.
Secrets held in fragrant dreams,
Nestled deep in nature's schemes.

As twilight deepens, magic from above,
Wraps each blossom, cradles each dove.
The garden sighs, a blissful retreat,
Where heartbeats and blossoms quietly meet.

Beneath the veil of the starlit night,
Dreams take flight in the silver light.
Each flower a story, whispered and bold,
In the quietude, mysteries unfold.

So linger awhile in this tranquil space,
Embrace the beauty, the soft, lingering grace.
For each whispering bloom in twilight's glow,
Holds the secrets only night could know.

Secrets of the Curved Branches

Beneath a canopy, the branches twist,
Curving gently, wrapped in mist.
Their tales are old, yet ever new,
Echoes of life in morning dew.

In the crooks where shadows play,
Secrets hide during the day.
Nature's whispers, soft and sweet,
Carried along by the rustling leaves.

Birds weave through, in joyful flight,
Sharing stories in the golden light.
The curved branches sway and bend,
In harmony with nature, they blend.

As dusk descends and colors merge,
The branches hum, a sacred dirge.
With every rustle, a call to see,
The wisdom of the living tree.

So come and listen to tales untold,
Under the branches, as night unfolds.
For in their curves, the world finds grace,
Secrets of life, in this sacred space.

Enchanted Lattice of Petals

In gardens woven with hues so bright,
Petals entwine in soft sunlight.
A lattice of color, a painter's dream,
Whispers of beauty in every seam.

The fragrance dances in the gentle air,
Each blossom sighs without a care.
A weave of magic, a tapestry fine,
Where nature's craftsman's designs entwine.

Dewdrops glisten on edges so clear,
Mirroring hopes that linger near.
As breezes brush, they sing a song,
Of love and life, where all belong.

As day gives way to the moon's embrace,
The lattice shimmers in twilight's grace.
Every petal whispers a story anew,
Beneath a canvas of stars and dew.

So wander through this enchanting space,
Where every corner holds nature's face.
In the lattice of petals, forever we roam,
Finding in beauty, our true home.

Beneath the Sapphire Skies

Underneath the vast sapphire dome,
Nature unfolds its boundless home.
Mountains rise and rivers flow,
With whispers of peace in every glow.

The azure stretch invites our gaze,
A canvas painted with sunlit rays.
Clouds drift softly, like thoughts in flight,
Dancing between day and night.

The golden warmth caresses the land,
Each grain of sand, delicate and grand.
Whispers of wind speak of freedom's quest,
In this tranquil haven, our souls find rest.

As twilight descends, the stars take their place,
The sky a tapestry, an endless embrace.
Beneath this vastness, we stand in awe,
Feeling the wonder, and nature's law.

So breathe in deeply, let your spirit soar,
Under sapphire skies, seek evermore.
For in this realm, where dreams intertwine,
The heart finds its rhythm, the soul in divine.

Celestial Dwellers of Nature's Embrace

In twilight's glow, the fireflies dance,
Soft whispers float, a fleeting chance.
Moonlit paths where shadows play,
The night unfolds in gentle sway.

Stars awaken, the heavens sigh,
Nature's breath beneath the sky.
Night blooms open, secrets free,
In this realm of mystery.

Frogs croak low in marshy tones,
Crickets strum their twilight drones.
Branches sway with the evening breeze,
Nature's heart, a lullaby's tease.

The river glimmers, a silver thread,
Softly cradling dreams long fled.
Each ripple tells a story bright,
In the magic of the night.

Celestial dwellers, moment's grace,
In harmony, we find our place.
With open hearts, we softly tread,
In this embrace, where dreams are led.

The Chronicles of Leafy Companions

Amidst the branches, stories weave,
Rustling leaves, where we believe.
Whispers carried on the breeze,
Tales of friendship among the trees.

Squirrels chatter, lively and free,
Jumping from branch to branch with glee.
Their laughter echoes, a playful sound,
In leafy realms where joy is found.

Beneath the shade, the stories grow,
Of ancient roots and streams that flow.
Each leaf a page, each bark a tale,
Chronicles swaying in nature's scale.

The rustle of ferns, the snap of twigs,
In silent woods where magic digs.
As seasons change, their stories bloom,
Painting the forest, a vibrant loom.

The sun dips low, in golden hues,
Embracing the night, with gentle views.
Together in silence, they softly hum,
The chronicles weave, forever come.

The Essence of Whispers Under the Stars

Beneath the vast expanse of night,
Whispers dance in soft twilight.
Stars like beacons in the dark,
Open souls, igniting spark.

Mountains watch with ancient eyes,
Guardians of our shared surprise.
In stillness, dreams begin to weave,
The essence of what we believe.

In shadows deep, where secrets lie,
The moonlight wanders, soft and shy.
Each twinkle tells of tales untold,
In the silken night, we are bold.

Rustling leaves, a melody sweet,
Nature's heartbeat, relatively discreet.
Under stars, where wishes soar,
Whispers echo forevermore.

The cosmos holds our silent fears,
Yet nurtures all our hidden tears.
In each moment, we find our peace,
The essence of life, a sweet release.

Silent Perches, Flourishing Tales

On silent perches, birds await,
With wise hearts, they contemplate.
Among the branches, stories bloom,
Flourishing tales, dispelling gloom.

Wings whisper secrets on the breeze,
Nature's hush held in the trees.
Each chirp a note in life's vast song,
Echoing where we all belong.

Clouds drift slowly, thoughts unspooled,
As colors blend, our hearts are schooled.
Lessons learned in skies so wide,
In silent perches where we confide.

The sun's warm rays, a gentle kiss,
In this stillness, we find our bliss.
Every moment, a new detail,
Whispers merge in flourishing tales.

Night descends, the world reflects,
In silent wonders, our hearts connect.
With every story, we find our place,
In nature's arms, a warm embrace.

Shadows of the Mystic Grove

Beneath the canopy of night,
Whispers dance in secret light,
Ancient trees in quiet pose,
Guard the tales that no one knows.

Shimmering stars like watchful eyes,
Guide the lost with silver sighs,
In the shadows, secrets dwell,
Nature's heart, a silent swell.

Branches weave a gentle maze,
Where the moonlight softly plays,
Echoes linger, soft and low,
In the depths of mystic woe.

Heartbeat of the earth resounds,
In the hush, a magic found,
Here the world turns slow and vast,
While the future blends with past.

Luminescent dreams take flight,
In the grove, the spirit's light,
Shadows merge in tranquil grace,
In this timeless, sacred space.

Dreams Entwined with Silken Vines

In a garden kissed by dawn,
Soft the threads of light are drawn,
Whispers weave through blooming air,
Dreams entwined, a tender snare.

Petals sigh in colors bright,
As the day unfolds its light,
Vines embrace with gentle hold,
Tales of love, in silence told.

Beneath the arch of emerald leaves,
Hearts find solace, hope believes,
In the shadows, secrets blend,
Where the journey has no end.

The fragrance drifts, a sweet allure,
Hearts entwined, so sweet and pure,
Each thread spun with dreams anew,
Woven tight, me and you.

As the sun begins to fade,
Magic lingers, softly laid,
In the twilight's soft embrace,
Dreams entwined, a sacred space.

Harmonies of the Forgotten Nest

In the quiet of the morn,
Songs of old are gently born,
Nestled high in branches strong,
Echoes of a world in song.

Feathers soft, in twilight's glow,
Whispers from the earth below,
Each note carries tales of yore,
In the heart, a silent roar.

Nature hums a timeless tune,
Underneath the watchful moon,
In the cradle of the trees,
Harmony rides on the breeze.

Lingering in dusk's embrace,
Memories of a sacred place,
Where the spirit learns to roam,
Finding solace, finding home.

The nest holds dreams both bright and vast,
In its warmth, the shadows cast,
Harmonies of those who've flown,
In this nest, we're never alone.

Moonlit Rituals in Leafy Hollows

In the hush of twilight's call,
Whispers rise and shadows fall,
Moonlit paths in leafy folds,
Tell the stories yet untold.

Candles flicker in the night,
Casting spells of soft delight,
Rituals of heart and soul,
In these hollows, we are whole.

Ancient spirits gather near,
In the stillness, feel the fear,
Yet in courage, light will spark,
Guided by the nature's arc.

Leaves entwine the sacred rite,
Underneath the silver light,
Each breath taken, deep and true,
In the moon's embrace, renew.

As the night begins to wane,
Magic lingers, sweet refrain,
In the hollows, dreams take flight,
Moonlit whispers, pure delight.

www.ingramcontent.com/pod-product-compliance
Ingram Content Group UK Ltd.
Pitfield, Milton Keynes, MK11 3LW, UK
UKHW021650200125
4194UKWH00003B/40